My F*CKING AWESOME BUCKET List

CIDER MILL PRESS

BOOK PUBLISHERS

#LIVEYOURLIST

13-Digit ISBN: 9781604336498
10-Digit ISBN: 1604336498

This book may be ordered by mail from the publisher. Please include $3.95 for postage and handling. Please support your local bookseller first!

Books published by Cider Mill Press Book Publishers are available at special discounts for bulk purchases in the United States by corporations, institutions, and other organizations. For more information, please contact the publisher.

Cider Mill Press Book Publishers
"Where good books are ready for press"
PO Box 454
12 Spring Street
Kennebunkport, Maine 04046

Visit us on the Web!
www.cidermillpress.com

Cover and interior design by Melissa Gerber

Typography: 1820 Modern, 2011 Slimtype, ATSackersGothic, Aachen, Adhesive Mr. Seven, Adobe Garamond, Agincourt, Algerian, Alternate Gothic, Amatic, Archer, Archistico, Archive Antique Extended, Archive Garfield, Archive Kludsky, Archive Old Style, Archive Roundface, Ashwood Condensed WF, Avenir, Betterfly, Birch, Bobbin, Bodoni, Botanica, Brandon, Bulmer, Burford, Caferus, Candy Script, Clarendon, Cloister, Comic Zine, Courier, DIN Cond, Dacquoise, Dead Man's Hand WF, EdPS Brush, Edwardian Script, Emmascript, Enjoy the Ride, Eveleth, Fenway Park, Festivo Letters, GFY Michael, Garamond 3, Ghost Type, Gist Rough, Great Vibes, Hellena Script, Hello Beautiful, Helvetica LT STD, Helvetica Neue, Helvetica Rounded, ITC Cheltenham, Kapra, Kathya, Kiln Serif, LHF Antique Shop, LHF Union Thug, Landscaper, Lemon Biscuit, Lobster, Local Market, Lulo, Macarons, Magnifico Daytime, Magnifico Nighttime, Manhattan Darling, Mercury Ornaments, Mesquite, Microbrew, Minion Pro, MrsEaves, NeoRetro, Nexa Rust, No. 1 type, No. 10 type, No. 11 type, No. 12 type, Pacific Northwest, Pontif, Populaire, Pricedown, Pringleton, Questa Grande, Requiem, Rosewood, Scrapbooker, Secret Service Typewriter, Sedgwick Co., SignPainter, Smaragd, Smoothy, Spirited Script, Sweet Sucker Punch, Thirsty, Trade Gothic, Trajan, Trend Slab, True North, Univers, Voyage, Wanderlust, Yonder, Zebrawood and Zurich.

All images used under official license from Shutterstock.com

Printed in China
1 2 3 4 5 6 7 8 9 0
First Edition

LIVE4OURLIST

You Have $100
TO MAKE TODAY

the most *Kick-Ass* day of your life.

COMPLETE THIS PIE CHART TO DESCRIBE HOW YOU'D ALLOCATE THE FUNDS.

#LIVEYOURLIST

YOU'VE JUST DIALED YOUR BOSS AND LEFT AN
ACADEMY-AWARD-WINNING
VOICEMAIL DETAILING YOUR RAGING CASE OF
"DENGUE FEVER." (Nice one, Bueller.)

HOW WILL YOU MAKE THE MOST OF PLAYING HOOKY TODAY?

6 A.M.	
7 A.M.	
8 A.M.	
9 A.M.	
10 A.M.	
11 A.M.	
12 P.M.	
1 P.M.	
2 P.M.	
3 P.M.	
4 P.M.	
5 P.M.	
6 P.M.	
7 P.M.	
8 P.M.	

#LIVEYOURLIST

WHO CARES IF A PICTURE'S WORTH A THOUSAND WORDS, WHEN SEEING SOMETHING IN PERSON CAN RENDER YOU DAMN NEAR SPEECHLESS?

LIST TEN THINGS YOU'D GIVE ANYTHING TO LAY EYES ON, BE IT THE SISTINE CHAPEL, HUGH HEFNER'S LEGENDARY GROTTO OR THE WORLD'S LARGEST BALL OF TWINE.

#LIVEYOURLIST

Compile a list of all of the activities that

ROCKED YOUR WORLD

when you were a kid.

Check at least five of those activities and go do them again.

[ ] SUMMER CAMP
[ ] SLUMBER PARTIES
[ ] EATING POP ROCKS
[ ] BIG WHEEL RACES
[ ] BUILDING A FORT
[ ] _____
[ ] _____
[ ] _____
[ ] _____
[ ] _____
[ ] _____

#LIVEYOURLIST

Sketch OR DESCRIBE A TATTOO YOU PLAN TO GET

→ YOU PLAN TO GET

(or would get if you weren't such a pussy about needles).

PINPOINT WHERE ON YOUR BODY YOU'D BE BRANDED.

LIVE YOUR LIST

Get nekkid.

CHECK OFF THE BOX FOR EACH LOCATION WHERE YOU'D BE PERFECTLY WILLING TO SHOW A LITTLE SKIN —

or a lot, as it were.

[ ] A NUDIST COLONY
[ ] A TOPLESS BEACH
[ ] MARDI GRAS
[ ] SKINNY DIPPING WITH FRIENDS
[ ] STREAKING THROUGH A PACKED FOOTBALL STADIUM
[ ] DINNER WITH THE IN-LAWS
[ ] A STRIP CLUB
[ ] A BODY-PAINTING FESTIVAL
[ ] A BATH HOUSE
[ ] BURNING MAN
[ ] MODELING FOR A CLASSROOM OF ART STUDENTS
[ ] A NIGHT SWIM IN YOUR NEIGHBOR'S POOL
[ ] NATURAL HOT SPRINGS
[ ] SAN FRANCISCO'S FETISH-CENTRIC FOLSOM STREET FAIR

#LIVEYOURLIST

Trust us,

you're going to be kicking yourself when you finally run out of time with them, so come up with twenty provocative and insightful questions to ask your parents.

BONUS:

Record your interview at NPR's StoryCorps at StoryCorps.org.

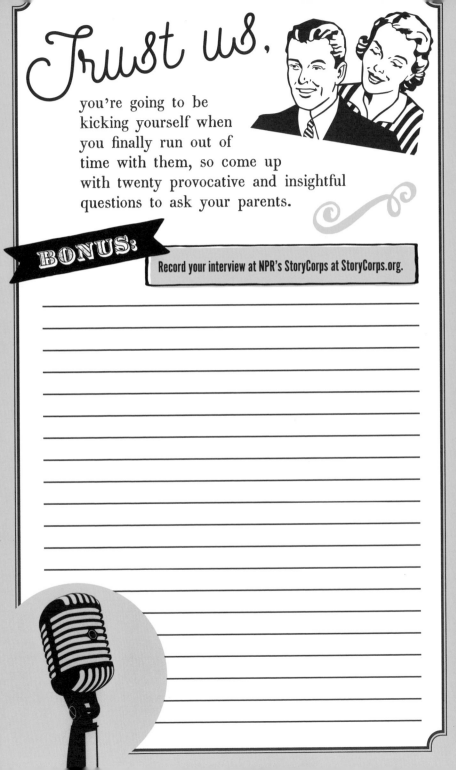

#LIVEYOURLIST

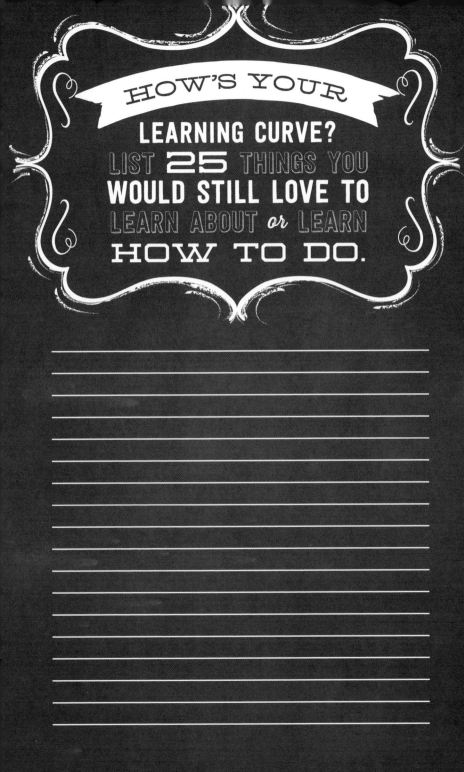

HOW'S YOUR

LEARNING CURVE?
LIST 25 THINGS YOU
WOULD STILL LOVE TO
LEARN ABOUT *or* LEARN
HOW TO DO.

#LIVEYOURLIST

Hold a color pen or marker 15 inches above this page, then drop it. Wherever it lands, plan to visit there before you die.

#LIVEYOURLIST

FUCK YOU,

Einstein!

If the laws of science no longer applied
for one day, what would you do?

_____

_____

_____

_____

_____

_____

_____

_____

_____

_____

_____

_____

#LIVEYOURLIST

COMMAND AN AUDIENCE

⋯ (and/or subject yourself to near–certain public humiliation) ⋯

BY COMPLETING THE INFORMATION BELOW,
THEN START CHECKING THEM OFF YOUR FUCKING AWESOME BUCKET LIST!

YOUR GO-TO KARAOKE TUNE:

THE TOPIC FOR YOUR FUTURE TED TALK:

Comic gold material for your stand-up bit:

A TUTORIAL YOU'D BE WILLING TO POST ON YOUTUBE:

The reason you'd most likely be interviewed by your local TV news station:

#LIVEYOURLIST

CONGRATULATIONS!

Your cousin Lester just hijacked a skywriting plane and has offered to etch your message to the world with his commandeered contrails. What would you have him write for all to see?

#LIVEYOURLIST

SO PIÑA COLADAS

And

GETTING CAUGHT IN

TORRENTIAL
DOWNPOURS

ISN'T YOUR THING?

FINE.

WHAT DO YOU CONSIDER TO BE LIFE'S
EMINENTLY AWESOME SIMPLE PLEASURES?

LIST THEM HERE.

#LIVEYOURLIST

"RAMBLE ON"

AS LED ZEPPELIN SO ELOQUENTLY ADVISED.

★ ★

FILL YOUR CAR'S GAS TANK, PICK A DIRECTION,
AND DRIVE AIMLESSLY UNTIL YOU NEED TO REFUEL.

WRITE ABOUT

WHERE YOU ENDED UP ON YOUR SOJOURN, OR PRINT
OUT THE LOCATION ON GOOGLE MAPS AND

PASTE IT HERE.

#LIVEYOURLIST

NEVER UNDERESTIMATE

The power

OF A PROVOCATIVE SPEECH, BE IT SHAKESPEARE'S "ST. CRISPIN'S DAY" BATTLE CRY OR BILL MURRAY'S "DALAI LAMA" SCHPIEL FROM CADDYSHACK.

What epically memorable poem, passage, or quotation will you commit to memory to impress colleagues, acquaintances, and potential love interests?

➤ ➤ **WRITE IT DOWN HERE.**

#LIVEYOURLIST

Deathbed

CONFESSION TIME:

What ten things in life do you think you'll wish you did more of? What ten things do you think you'll wish you did less of?

_____   _____

_____   _____

_____   _____

_____   _____

_____   _____

_____   _____

_____   _____

_____   _____

_____   _____

_____   _____

#LIVEYOURLIST

What WORLD RECORD
WOULD YOU LOVE TO BREAK BEFORE YOU DIE?

Design your own "Evil Knievel" worthy costume to don while you astonish and amaze with your feats of derring-do.

Design Your Costume

Death defying stunt!

#LIVEYOURLIST

COLOR IN
ALL OF THE STATES

you've already been to, then rank, in order of
preference, the states you would want to visit next.

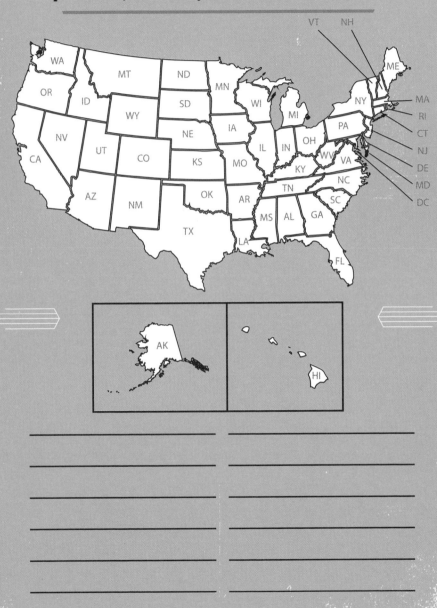

#LIVEYOURLIST

[BIGGEST *fucking*]

REGRETS IN THE CORRECT COLUMNS.

Things I Can Remedy

Things To Let Go

#LIVEYOURLIST

YOU HAVE

$100,000

TO MAKE TODAY *THE* MOST KICK-ASS DAY OF YOUR LIFE.

COMPLETE THIS PIE CHART TO DESCRIBE HOW YOU'D ALLOCATE THE FUNDS.

#LIVEYOURLIST

LIST ALL OF THE BANDS
YOU WANT TO SEE LIVE BEFORE YOU DIE.

Paste the ticket
stubs here once
you've seen them.

_____

_____

_____

_____

_____

_____

_____

_____

_____

_____

_____

#LIVEYOURLIST

List five things
(OR, OKAY, PEOPLE)
YOU'D LOVE TO

RIDE

BEFORE YOU DIE.

[   ] A DUCATI MOTORCYCLE

[   ] A CAMEL

[   ] A MECHANICAL BULL

[   ] A SEGWAY

[   ] A ROSE BOWL FLOAT

[   ] A MOTORIZED SHOPPING CART
     AT THE GROCERY STORE

_____

_____

_____

_____

TICKET

#LIVEYOURLIST

IF YOU WERE GOING TO WRITE
THE STORY OF YOUR LIFE,

or the

"GREAT AMERICAN NOVEL,"

WHAT WOULD BE THE TITLE,
PREMISE, AND OPENING PARAGRAPH?

#LIVEYOURLIST

FOR ONE WEEK, TRY OUT SOMETHING YOU WOULD NORMALLY SAVAGELY MOCK,

LIKE GROWING A HANDLEBAR MUSTACHE OR LISTENING TO YANNI.

Did your experience change your opinion at all?

#LIVEYOURLIST

LIST FIVE

of your

AWFUL HABITS

and circle at least one that you are committed to kicking,

STARTING TODAY.

1. _____

2. _____

3. _____

4. _____

5. _____

#LIVEYOURLIST

#LIVEYOURLIST

WRITE A DESCRIPTION FOR YOUR DREAM JOB.

JOB TITLE:

BASIC DUTIES:

SKILLS REQUIRED:

STARTING SALARY:

HOURS PER WEEK:

BENEFITS:

PREREQUISITES AND BONUSES:

#LIVEYOURLIST

What would you do in the following amounts of time left on Earth?

One day: _____

One week: _____

One month: _____

One year: _____

#LIVEYOURLIST

List five

"BUCKET LIST"

AMBITIONS FOR EACH OF THE FOLLOWING CATEGORIES.

(Don't worry, we won't tell Santa.)

Naughty   *Nice*

_____   _____

_____   _____

_____   _____

_____   _____

_____   _____

#LIVEYOURLIST

Sketch the exterior or draw a blueprint *for your* FUCKING AWESOME dream home.

#LIVEYOURLIST

Defy GRAVITY

CHECK OFF AT LEAST ONE OF THE FOLLOWING ACTIVITIES TO CROSS OFF YOUR BUCKET LIST.

[ ] BUNGEE JUMP

[ ] GO ZIP-LINING

[ ] VOLUNTEER TO HELP COLONIZE MARS

[ ] FLY IN A HELICOPTER

[ ] RIDE IN A HOT AIR BALLOON

[ ] SKYDIVE

[ ] WALK ON STILTS

[ ] TAKE TRAPEZE LESSONS

[ ] BASE JUMP

[ ] JUMP FROM ONE ROOFTOP TO
    ANOTHER, JASON BOURNE-STYLE

[ ] CLIMB THE SYDNEY HARBOR BRIDGE

[ ] VISIT A TRAMPOLINE PARK

[ ] GO OVER NIAGARA FALLS
    IN A BARREL

[ ] WALK A TIGHTROPE

[ ] GO ROCK CLIMBING

#LIVEYOURLIST

THROW A DRINK

**WHO WOULD THEY BE, AND WHAT WOULD
YOU SAY TO THEM WHILE DOING IT?**

_____

_____

_____

_____

_____

_____

_____

_____

_____

_____

_____

_____

#LIVE4OURLIST

CLASSIC BOOKS.

They're not just for crusty-looking librarians.

Strike through the ones you've already read and circle the ones on your "want to read" list. Then add your own aspirational classic reads.

Alice's Adventures in Wonderland by Lewis Carroll
Invisible Man by Ralph Ellison
Ulysses by James Joyce
Moby Dick by Herman Melville
Don Quixote by Miguel de Cervantes
Anna Karenina by Leo Tolstoy
The Great Gatsby by F. Scott Fitzgerald
Pride and Prejudice by Jane Austen
One Hundred Years of Solitude by Gabriel Garcia Marquez
To Kill a Mockingbird by Harper Lee
Hamlet by William Shakespeare
Catch-22 by Joseph Heller
Beloved by Toni Morrison
Jane Eyre by Charlotte Bronte
Les Misérables by Victor Hugo

_____

_____

_____

_____

_____

#LIVEYOURLIST

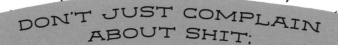

DON'T JUST COMPLAIN ABOUT SHIT:

DO SOMETHING ABOUT IT.

NAME A SOCIAL INJUSTICE, OUTRAGEOUS INEQUITY, OR ANNOYING PET PEEVE YOU'D LOVE TO ABOLISH AND DESCRIBE HOW YOU WOULD GHANDI THE CRAP OUT OF IT.

_____

_____

_____

_____

_____

_____

_____

#LIVEYOURLIST

BURY THE HATCHET.

CHOOSE ONE PERSON WHO'S CURRENTLY ON YOUR SHIT LIST
AND DESCRIBE HOW YOU MIGHT ATTEMPT TO BROKER PEACE.

#LIVEYOURLIST

COOK

*at least one new dish
(or sample a new delicacy)
every month for the next year.*

RECORD YOUR CULINARY ADVENTURES HERE.

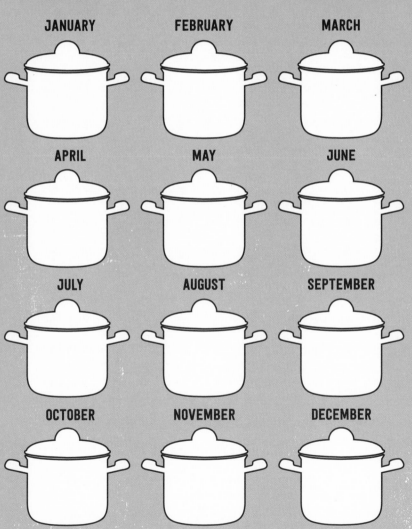

JANUARY

FEBRUARY

MARCH

APRIL

MAY

JUNE

JULY

AUGUST

SEPTEMBER

OCTOBER

NOVEMBER

DECEMBER

#LIVEYOURLIST

WRITE A LETTER THANKING THE INDIVIDUAL YOU MOST CREDIT WITH MAKING YOU AS FUCKING AWESOME A PERSON AS YOU ARE.

#LIVEYOURLIST

"Why the hell did you waste so much money on that?"

Prompt someone in your life to say exactly that by going for broke on a crazy, stupid splurge.

What would you spring for?

$800

$6,500

$1,200

_____

_____

_____

_____

_____

_____

#LIVEYOURLIST

IMAGINE YOU'VE BEEN INVITED
BACK TO YOUR ALMA MATER TO GIVE
THE COMMENCEMENT ADDRESS.

What advice would you give these clueless newbies?

#LIVEYOURLIST

TO TELL FUTURE
GENERATIONS
ABOUT HOW
 # AWESOME
YOU ONCE WERE.

_____   _____

_____   _____

_____   _____

_____   _____

_____   _____

_____   _____

_____   _____

_____   _____

LIVE4OURLIST

WHEN A DOUBLE
RAINBOW
CAN MOVE A GROWN MAN TO TEARS,
THAT'S THE POWER OF NATURE.

LIST ALL OF THE WORLD'S NATURAL WONDERS
YOU'D LOVE TO SEE BEFORE YOU DIE.

_____

_____

_____

_____

_____

_____

_____

_____

LIVE4OURLIST

Use this SPACE TO write a MESSAGE SEND To in a bottle.

THEN DECIDE IF YOU'RE REALLY THE SORT OF A-HOLE WHO LITTERS OUR MAJESTIC OCEANS WITH USED DRINK RECEPTACLES. IF YOU ARE, THEN GO AHEAD AND SEND IT!

#LIVEYOURLIST

LIST 10 COUNTRIES
WHERE YOU'D LIKE
TO TRY LIVING FOR
AT LEAST SIX MONTHS.

_____

_____

_____

_____

_____

_____

_____

_____

_____

_____

#LIVEYOURLIST

PLAN THE

ULTIMATE
ROAD TRIP.

WHO WOULD GO WITH YOU, WHERE WOULD
YOU GO, AND WHAT TUNES WOULD BE
REQUIRED LISTENING EN ROUTE? MAP OUT
YOUR COMPLETE JOURNEY HERE.

passengers   destinations   songs

#LIVEYOURLIST

RUNNING WITH BULLS?
SWIMMING WITH SHARKS?
WALKING INTO A BIKER BAR?

MAKE A LIST OF ACTIVITIES THAT WOULD MAKE YOU PISS YOUR PANTS (OR WORSE), THEN CIRCLE THREE YOU WILL MUSTER THE COURAGE TO TRY.

#LIVEYOURLIST

DO SOMETHING CRAZY

IN THE NAME OF CHARITY

LIKE JUMPING INTO FREEZING WATER, SHAVING YOUR HEAD, OR DYEING YOUR EYEBROWS HOT PINK. DESCRIBE WHAT YOU CHOSE, HOW MUCH MONEY YOU EARNED, AND FOR WHICH CHARITY.

_____

_____

_____

_____

#LIVEYOURLIST

There's a lot *OF* WEIRD *shit* OUT THERE,

AS EVIDENCED BY MUSEUMS AROUND THE GLOBE DEDICATED TO CONDOMS, INSTANT RAMEN, BUNNY PARAPHERNALIA, ALLEGED AXE-MURDERER LIZZIE BORDEN, AND TOILETS.

Research and list five bizarre museums you would like to visit.

_____

_____

_____

_____

_____

#LIVEYOURLIST

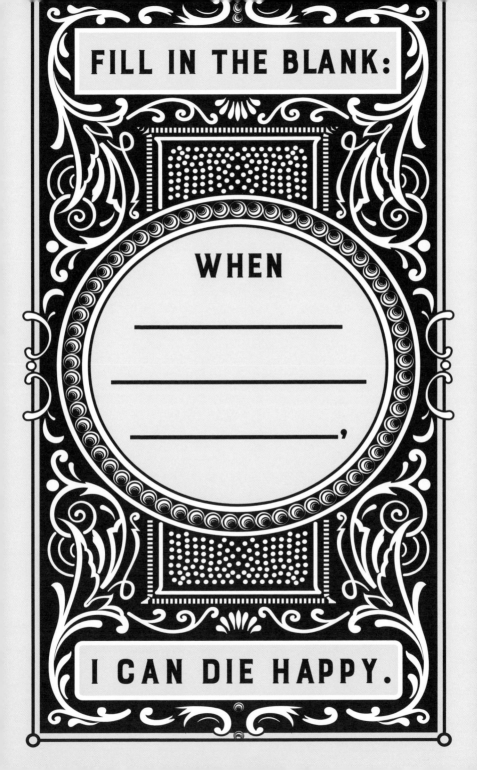

FILL IN THE BLANK:

WHEN

_____

_____

_____,

I CAN DIE HAPPY.

#LIVEYOURLIST

"I NEVER..."

LIST THIRTY RELATIVELY COMMONPLACE ACTIVITIES YOU'VE NEVER EXPERIENCED. CROSS THEM OFF AS YOU EVENTUALLY GIVE 'EM THE OLD COLLEGE TRY.

#LIVEYOURLIST

WHAT WOULD YOU DO?

#LIVEYOURLIST

IF YOU HAD AN OPPORTUNITY TO GO BACK TO SCHOOL,

WHAT WOULD YOU CHOOSE TO STUDY?

_____

_____

_____

_____

_____

_____

_____

_____

#LIVEYOURLIST

LIST PERSONAL AMBITIONS FOR EVERY LETTER OF THE ALPHABET.

(AND YEAH... GOOD LUCK WITH "X AND Z")

A _____

B _____

C _____

D _____

E _____

F _____

G _____

H _____

I _____

J _____

K _____

L _____

M _____

N _____

O _____

P _____

Q _____

R _____

S _____

T _____

U _____

V _____

W _____

X _____

Y _____

Z _____

#LIVEYOURLIST

Live these clichés:

TAKE A SLOW BOAT TO CHINA

BET YOUR BOTTOM DOLLAR

BLOW SMOKE UP SOMEONE'S ASS

CATCH SOMEONE WITH THEIR PANTS DOWN

TEACH AN OLD DOG NEW TRICKS

CRACK A WHIP

STOP AND SMELL THE ROSES

_____

_____

_____

_____

_____

_____

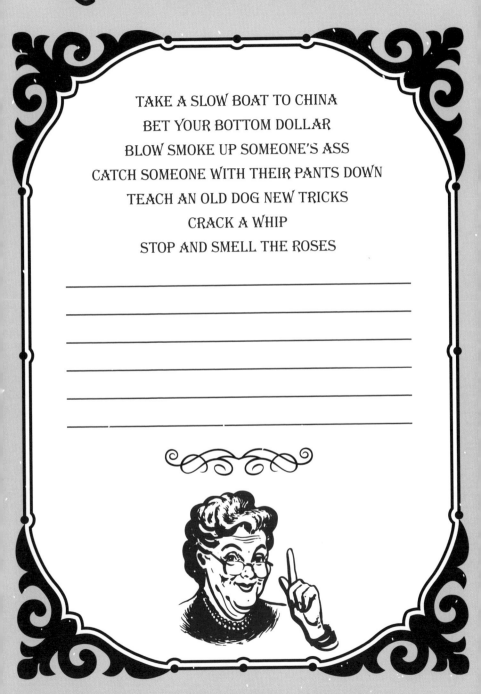

#LIVEYOURLIST

THINK OF TEN CRAZY WAYS TO ANONYMOUSLY MAKE A COMPLETE STRANGER'S DAY BY SPENDING LESS THAN $20.

(THEN GO DO ONE OF THEM, YOU JERK!)

1

2

3

4

5

6

7

8

9

10

#LIVEYOURLIST

LEARN TO *make* AT LEAST FIVE OF *the* FOLLOWING

CLASSIC COCKTAILS.

STRIKE THROUGH THE REST AS YOU'VE SAMPLED THEM.

[ ] Sidecar
[ ] Manhattan
[ ] Rob Roy
[ ] Whiskey Sour
[ ] Gin Fizz
[ ] Gimlet
[ ] Negroni
[ ] Old Fashioned
[ ] Moscow Mule
[ ] Martini
[ ] Mint Julep
[ ] Dark 'n Stormy
[ ] Margarita
[ ] Mojito
[ ] Boulevardier
[ ] Vieux Carré

#LIVEYOURLIST

WOULD *you* RATHER...?

(mark an "x" next to your preference)

[ ] Kiss a stranger or kiss an old flame? [ ]
[ ] Climb Mt. Everest or ride in a submarine? [ ]
[ ] Attend your high school reunion or go on a vacation by yourself? [ ]
[ ] Visit the Great Barrier Reef or see the Great Wall of China? [ ]
[ ] Learn the tango or the Texas Two Step? [ ]
[ ] Go on a blind date or to a business convention? [ ]
[ ] Have a personal chef or a maid? [ ]
[ ] Be too busy or too bored? [ ]
[ ] Visit Antarctica or the Sahara Desert? [ ]
[ ] Play for a professional sports team or own a professional sports team? [ ]
[ ] Own your own yacht or own a private jet? [ ]
[ ] Have nine children or no children? [ ]
[ ] End hunger or hatred? [ ]
[ ] Be filthy rich or find the love of your life? [ ]
[ ] Give up the Internet or give up your car? [ ]

#LIVEYOURLIST

HITTING UP EVERY NATIONAL PARK, MAJOR LEAGUE BASEBALL STADIUM, OR CITY IN JOHNNY CASH'S CLASSIC "I'VE BEEN EVERYWHERE"?

Plot out your multi-pronged pilgrimage ideas here.

_____

_____

_____

_____

_____

_____

_____

_____

_____

_____

#LIVEYOURLIST

"COME ON DOWN."

"YABBA DABBA DOO."

"Whatchootalkin-boutWillis?"

Coin your own catchphrase.
Brainstorm your ideas here.

_____
_____
_____
_____
_____
_____
_____
_____
_____
_____
_____
_____
_____

#LIVEYOURLIST

To what famous person would you send a fan letter? Channel your inner uber-geek and write it here.

#LIVEYOURLIST

FUCKING AWESOME TALENTS

DESERVE TO BE PASSED ON TO FUTURE GENERATIONS.

WHAT SKILLS OR TALENTS ARE YOU BEST EQUIPPED TO PASS ON TO A PROTÉGÉ?

_____
_____
_____
_____
_____
_____
_____

#LIVEYOURLIST

YOU'D LOVE TO SNEAK INTO AFTER HOURS FOR ONE NIGHT.

_____
_____
_____
_____
_____

_____
_____
_____
_____
_____

#LIVEYOURLIST

STRIKE UP
A CONVERSATION

with **EVERY** → **STRANGER YOU COME ACROSS TODAY. WRITE ABOUT THE MOST INTERESTING INDIVIDUAL YOU MET.**

#LIVEYOURLIST

IT'S TIME TO
RELINQUISH YOUR FATE
TO SOMEONE ELSE.

Ask ten friends, relatives, or acquaintances to each fill in a line below with a bucket list goal for you to accomplish. (You can thank us, or kill us, later.)

NAME

NAME

NAME

NAME

NAME

NAME

NAME

NAME

NAME

NAME

#LIVEYOURLIST

TRY ONE NEW THING

(be it perfectly mundane or life-changingly amazeballs)

EVERY WEEK FOR ONE YEAR.

#LIVEYOURLIST

"PARTY LIKE A ROCK STAR,"

WHAT, EXACTLY, WOULD THAT ENTAIL?

ROCK

STAR

#LIVEYOURLIST

IF YOU COULD SPEARHEAD A NEW CHARITY IN YOUR NAME, WHAT CAUSE WOULD YOU CHAMPION?

HOW WOULD YOUR ORGANIZATION HELP?

_____

_____

_____

_____

_____

_____

_____

_____

_____

#LIVEYOURLIST

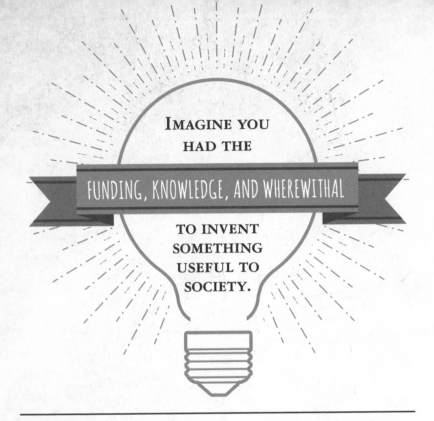

IMAGINE YOU
HAD THE

FUNDING, KNOWLEDGE, AND WHEREWITHAL

TO INVENT
SOMETHING
USEFUL TO
SOCIETY.

DESCRIBE OR DRAW YOUR INVENTION AND WHAT IT DOES.

#LIVEYOURLIST

List all of the JOURNEYS. YOU'D LOVE to take on foot

[ ] THE ROAD TO MACHU PICCHU

[ ] THE APPALACHIAN TRAIL

[ ] THE GREAT WALL OF CHINA

[ ] HOLLYWOOD'S WALK OF FAME

[ ] CLIMBING MOUNT KILIMANJARO

[ ] DESCENDING INTO THE GRAND CANYON

[ ] BOSTON'S FREEDOM TRAIL

[ ] _____
[ ] _____
[ ] _____
[ ] _____
[ ] _____
[ ] _____
[ ] _____
[ ] _____

#LIVEYOURLIST

#LIVEYOURLIST

IF YOU WERE GOING TO START **A BUSINESS OR ENTERPRISE** OF YOUR OWN, WHAT WOULD IT BE?

DRAW YOUR TOTALLY AWESOME LOGO OR INSIGNIA BELOW.

#LIVEYOURLIST

CREATE
A MUSIC
PLAYLIST
THAT BEST
SUMMARIZES
YOUR LIFE.

#LIVEYOURLIST

WHAT NATIONALLY OR INTERNATIONALLY TELEVISED EVENT WOULD YOU LOVE TO ATTEND IN PERSON?

MAYBE THE OSCARS®,
AN OLYMPIC GAMES
OPENING CEREMONY,
OR PERHAPS

The

SUPERBOWL?

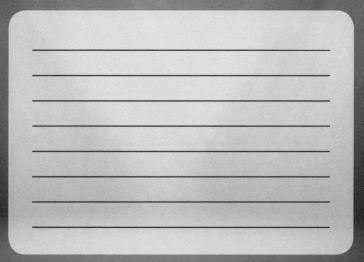

#LIVEYOURLIST

NAME FIVE LONG-LOST FRIENDS
(OR OLD FLAMES)

from your past whom you still think about, then do a little cyber-stalking to see if you can determine where they're at and what they're up to today.

#LIVEYOURLIST

Plan your own flash mob.

WHERE WOULD YOU STAGE IT

AND WHAT WOULD THE PERFORMANCE ENTAIL?

_____

_____

_____

_____

_____

_____

#LIVEYOURLIST

GAME MATCH-UP
YOU DREAM ABOUT SEEING
BEFORE YOUR OWN PERSONAL
GAME CLOCK
EXPIRES.

MMXIV

VS

#LIVEYOURLIST

WHAT WOULD YOU WANT TO SAY TO YOUR BOSS ON YOUR LAST DAY ON THE JOB?

Write it here.

#LIVEYOURLIST

What game shows or reality shows would you love to be a contestant on?

_____

_____

_____

_____

_____

_____

_____

_____

#LIVEYOURLIST

Compile a list

OF THE REAL-LIFE
movie Meccas
YOU'D LOVE
TO VISIT IN PERSON.

[ ] IOWA'S "FIELD OF DREAMS"
[ ] THE GOONIES' HOUSE IN ASTORIA, OREGON
[ ] RALPHIE'S HOUSE FROM A CHRISTMAS STORY IN CLEVELAND, OHIO
[ ] THE WIZARDING WORLD OF HARRY POTTER AT UNIVERSAL STUDIOS
[ ] THE LORD OF THE RINGS SHIRE SET IN MATAMATA, NEW ZEALAND
[ ] THE SHINING'S STANLEY HOTEL IN ESTES PARK, COLORADO
[ ] _____
[ ] _____
[ ] _____
[ ] _____
[ ] _____
[ ] _____

#LIVEYOURLIST

Practicality is the buzzkill of dreams. List 20 frivolous, foolish, and completely impractical things you'd like to do before you die.

_____
_____
_____
_____
_____
_____
_____
_____
_____
_____
_____
_____
_____
_____
_____
_____
_____
_____
_____
_____

#LIVEYOURLIST

. . . But how, exactly, are you going to get that cow up on the roof?

NEVER MIND. JUST MAKE A LIST OF PRACTICAL JOKES YOU'D LOVE TO PLAY ON SOMEONE BEFORE YOU CHECK OUT.

#LIVEYOURLIST

If the rules OF MONOGAMY WERE SUSPENDED For one night,

WHICH TEN PEOPLE WOULD YOU WANT TO SLEEP WITH?

#LIVEYOURLIST

IF YOU COULD USE A
TIME MACHINE TO VISIT ANY
PREVIOUS ERA, WHAT TIME
PERIOD WOULD YOU TRAVEL
TO? SINCE TIME TRAVEL ISN'T
ACTUALLY POSSIBLE, HOW
MIGHT YOU RECREATE THAT
ERA IN HISTORY?

#LIVEYOURLIST

COMPLETE THE
FOLLOWING SENTENCE
WITH
AS MANY APPROPRIATE
RESPONSES
AS YOU CAN THINK OF:

{ "LIFE IS TOO FUCKING SHORT TO LIVE WITHOUT _____." }

#LIVEYOURLIST

IF YOU HAD AN OPPORTUNITY TO TALK TO YOUR YOUNGER SELF ON A PARK BENCH FOR ONE HOUR, WHAT ADVICE WOULD YOU HAVE FOR THAT **LITTLE SHIT**?

#LIVEYOURLIST

List ten romantic
things you'd like to
do for someone, and
list ten romantic
things you'd love
someone else to
do for you.

#LIVEYOURLIST

NAME TEN OF THE WORLD'S MOST

badass people

(real or fictional, living or deceased)

WHOM YOU ASPIRE TO EMULATE IN SOME WAY.

#LIVEYOURLIST

Write down the names of the first 10 people you know who come to mind.

_____

_____

_____

_____

_____

_____

_____

_____

_____

_____

{ *Call each person today to tell them why you think they are fucking awesome.* }

#LIVEYOURLIST

FINISH

ALL OF
SOMETHING,
WHETHER
THAT MEANS
READING THE
COMPLETE
WORKS OF
SHAKESPEARE,
WATCHING
EVERY
EPISODE OF
THE WIRE, OR
CONQUERING
EVERY LEVEL
IN CANDY
CRUSH SAGA.

"I VOW TO COMPLETE

_____

IN ITS ENTIRETY."

LIVEYOURLIST

IF YOU WERE GOING TO BEQUEATH A LARGE FORTUNE TO THE WORLD UPON YOUR DEATH, HOW WOULD YOU LIKE THOSE FUNDS TO BE SPENT? WHAT STIPULATIONS, IF ANY, WOULD YOU ATTACH TO YOUR DONATION?

DONATION

STIPULATIONS

#LIVEYOURLIST

THAT JESUS GUY WAS ON TO SOMETHING. PLAN YOUR OWN "LAST SUPPER." WHO WOULD YOU INVITE, AND WHAT'S ON THE MENU?

GUEST LIST

_____ _____ _____

MENU

#LIVEYOURLIST

IF YOU COULD BE

immortalized

IN STATUE FORM,

SKETCH OUT HOW YOU WOULD
LIKE TO BE DEPICTED.

#LIVEYOURLIST

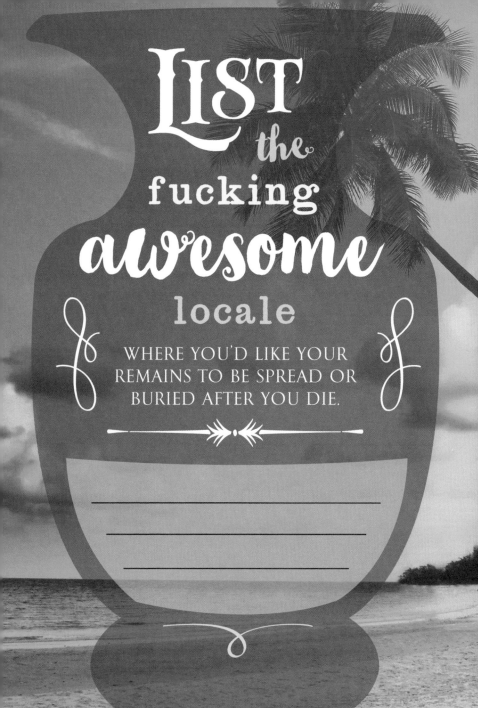

LIST
the
fucking
awesome
locale

WHERE YOU'D LIKE YOUR
REMAINS TO BE SPREAD OR
BURIED AFTER YOU DIE.

_____

_____

_____

#LIVEYOURLIST

WHAT "STUPID HUMAN TRICK" WOULD YOU LIKE TO PERFECT?

#LIVEYOURLIST

#LIVEYOURLIST

ARE YOU UP FOR

RUNNING A MARATHON?
CYCLING FROM MAINE TO FLORIDA?
EATING THE 72 OZ.
STEAK AT THE BIG TEXAN
IN AMARILLO, TEXAS?

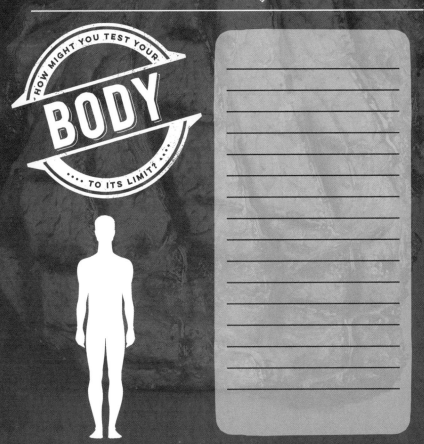

HOW MIGHT YOU TEST YOUR
BODY
TO ITS LIMIT?

#LIVEYOURLIST

#LIVEYOURLIST

No one can cheat death forever,

but it probably wouldn't suck quite so bad if you could choose to go out in a blaze of glory. Describe your ideal scenario for saying your final ten-four to the good people of the world.

#LIVEYOURLIST

DESIGN YOUR OWN
TOMBSTONE.

#LIVEYOURLIST

WRITE YOUR OWN OBITUARY AS IF
YOU HAD LIVED YOUR IDEAL LIFE.

OBITUARY

#LIVEYOURLIST

BE A FUCKING GROWN-UP.

Write a list of the most responsible
things you can do in your life.

- Have a 401k
- Know your credit score
- Invest in something cool

_____
_____
_____
_____
_____
_____

#LIVEYOURLIST

ONCE YOU FINALLY DO KICK THE BUCKET, WHO DO YOU HOPE TO MEET ON THE OTHER SIDE? WHAT DO YOU HOPE THEY SAY ABOUT YOU?

_____

_____

_____

_____

_____

#LIVEYOURLIST